Why I Thank God

Grace Young

WestBow Press books may be ordered through booksellers or by contacting:

WestBow Press
A Division of Thomas Nelson & Zondervan
1663 Liberty Drive
Bloomington, IN 47403
www.westbowpress.com
844-714-3454

ISBN: 978-1-6642-5078-9 (sc)
ISBN: 978-1-6642-5079-6 (e)

Library of Congress Control Number: 2021923747

Print information available on the last page.

WestBow Press rev. date: 2/21/2022

WestBow
PRESS®
A DIVISION OF THOMAS NELSON
& ZONDERVAN

This story is about a little boy who owes all of his blessings to God. He comes from a religious family. He doesn't quite have a full understanding of God yet, but he does know that He exists. He is very thankful for the blessings he has received.

This book is dedicated to Tracey, Crystal, Michele, and Larmont Young Jr.

I thank God for the sun that shines.

I thank God for the
pretty blue sky.

I thank God for the
birds that sing.

I thank God for the pretty flowers.

I thank God for my brother.

I thank God for my sister.

I thank God for my
mother and father.

I thank God for my cat.

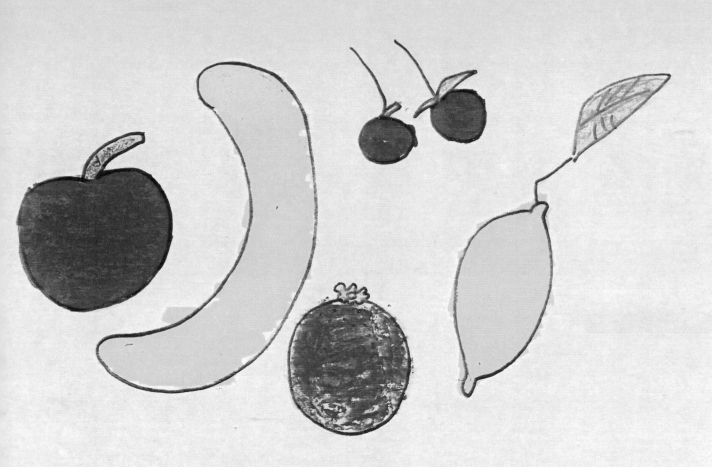

I thank God for the food we eat.

I thank God for the clothes we wear.

I thank God
for the trees.

I thank God for my church.

I thank
God for
my school.

I thank
God for my
house.

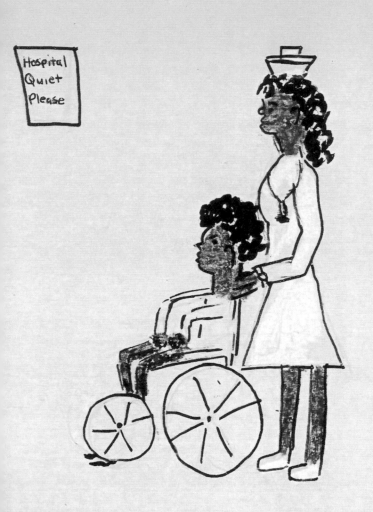

I thank God for the doctors and nurses.

And last but not least,
I thank God for me.

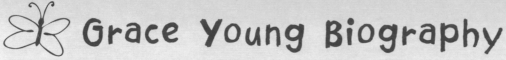 Grace Young Biography

Grace Elizabeth (Williams) Young, I was born in Port Chester, New York and attended the Port Chester Rye Brook Public School System and graduated from the Port Chester High School in 1968. I am a widow and was married to Mr. Larmont Young, from Tuckahoe, New York who passed away in 1980. We have four children, Tracey, Crystral, Michele, and Larmont Young Jr.

I earned my Bachelor's Degree in Psychology with minor in Elementary Education and a Master of Science Degree in Education (Reading). I also hold permanent certificates in Education and Reading from the College of New Rochelle and a certificate of Theology from Oral Roberts University in Tulsa, Oklahoma. I also earned an A.A.S. Degree in Nursing from Pace University in Pleasantville, New York.

I started working for the Port Chester Rye Brook School System in 1977 as a Substitute Teacher and did so for 13 years. I was a teacher of Adult Basic Education in Math and Reading from 1974–1977, and I also taught kindergarten at Thomas A. Edison Elementary School for a few years. I have been a substitute nurse for the District and also a tutor. I held the following position for the next 23 years as a Reading Specialist at Corpus Christi-Holy Rosary School until I retired in 2013.

I am very active in the Port Chester Community. I am a member of the American Red Cross Disaster Services and have been a member for 25 years. I have held various positions with them such as: First Aid and C.P.R. Instructor, Disaster Services Nurse, Sound the Alarm, distributing fire alarms, Blood Donor Ambassador, Hurricane Katrina, and Hurricane Sandy, working in the shelters. I am still presently involved with them. I am a member of the Port Chester Teachers Association. I am also a member of W.E.V. R. C. (Westchester Emergency Volunteer Reserve Corp) as a volunteer nurse. I was a volunteer at United Hospital in the Emergency Room until the hospital closed in 2005. I was also a volunteer at the Greenwich Hospital in the Emergency Room. I was also an E.M.T. (Emergency Medical Technician) and worked at Playland, in Rye, New York. I also volunteered with Harrison Volunteer Ambulance Corp., in Harrison, New York.

I am a member of St. Frances A.M.E. Zion Church, where I held the following positions (Chairman of the Trustee Board) from the year 2012 for six years, Assistant Superintendent of the Sunday School, a Sunday School Teacher, W.H.O.M. (Women's Home and Overseas Mission Society), Church Health Medical Staff Member as a nurse. I have been volunteering in the church soup kitchen for over 25 years and also participated as a volunteer at Corpus Christi Church for the Midnight Run (a program that goes out and feeds the homeless who are living in the streets and handing out food and clothing). I am also a member of the N.A.A.C.P.

I am also a volunteer at Don Bosco, Community Center with their outreach program passing out food and clothing to the needy.

I received Proclamations October 15, 2016 from the following: Westchester County Board of Legislators, Port Chester, New York, Town of Rye Westchester County New York, Port Chester-Rye N.A.A.C.P., Freedom Fund Luncheon Award Meritorious Activities received awards from George Latimer, New York State Senate, New York State Assembly Citation. (State Assemblyman) Steven Otis, Office of County Executive Westchester County, New York, Robert Asterino, (County Executive) Award, and Honorary Teacher Retirement of Outstanding Accomplishments June 19, 2013 (Superintendent of Schools) Dr. Edward Kliszus.

Award Certificate: With the American Red Cross for 25 years of service volunteering I received a Citation March 25, 2021 from Assemblyman, Steven Otis.

I am the proud grandmother of seven grandchildren and four great grandchildren. In my leisure time I love reading, dabbling in clay arts, bicycle riding, ice skating and walking on nice days.

I strongly believe that the children are our future. I believe in what the Bible says (Proverbs 22: 6) "Train up a child in the way he should go: and when he is old, he will not depart from it."